A Little Chinese Cookbook

Terry Tan

ILLUSTRATED BY SUSAN DRAY

First published in 1990 by
The Appletree Press Ltd, 7 James Street South,
Belfast BT2 8DL.
Copyright © 1990 The Appletree Press, Ltd. Illustrations ©
1990 Susan Dray used under Exclusive License to
The Appletree Press, Ltd.
Printed in Hong Kong. All rights reserved.

British Library Cataloguing in Publication Data
Tan, Terry
A Little Chinese Cookbook
1. Food, Chinese dishes. Recipes
I. Title
641.5951

ISBN: 0-86281-253-4

First published in the United States in 1990
by Chronicle Books, 275 Fifth Street,
San Francisco, CA 94103

ISBN 0-87701-798-8

9 8 7 6 5 4 3 2 1

Introduction

While Chinese cuisine is universally popular, it has the undeserved reputation of being intimidating. Those 'mystifying sauces' are easily available in stores. As for methods and utensils, this book will de-mystify them. The Ying Yang philosophy that permeates Chinese life is evident in its cuisine, giving a balance of opposite elements – dark and light, soft and crunchy, sweet and sour. The result should be a feeling of wellbeing after a meal. No two Chinese chefs ever cook the same dish the same way, each creates his own flavours. Whether attempting an imperial Peking Duck or humble peasant stew, approach it with a sense of adventure and boldness. It's a matter of trial, and a few errors, before you know the perfect harmony between ginger and sesame oil, plum sauce and vinegar, soy sauce and garlic, noodles and beansprouts and the endless permutations therein. A Chinese meal for four consists of two or three dishes served with rice. All dishes will serve two or more if the meal includes other dishes, unless otherwise indicated. A meal for four can easily be stretched by serving more rice.

A note on measures

Imperial, metric and American measures have been used in this book. Use one set of measures only as they are not necessarily exact equivalents. The cup referred to is the standard American measure, and spoon measures are level, not heaped. All recipes will serve four people.

Savoury Tossed Chicken Noodles

Bread is not truly a part of Chinese cuisine and breakfast is really pot luck. Mostly a simplified version of lunch or dinner, it draws from a wide range of single-portion rice and noodle-based dishes. 4 oz/100 g noodles is ample for one.

---

4 oz/100 g dry egg noodles
3 tbsp vegetable oil
6 oz/150 g/¾ cup chicken breast
1 stalk celery
1 oz/25 g/2 tbsp dark soy sauce
½ tsp ground black pepper
8 fl oz/250 ml/1 cup water
1 chicken stock cube
2 stalks spring onions, chopped

Cook noodles to packet instructions. Drain and loosen strands. Slice chicken into thin strips. Slice celery on the diagonal ¾ in/1 cm wide. Heat oil in wok or frying pan until smoking and add chicken, stirring vigorously until meat turns opaque. Add celery, soy sauce, pepper, water and stock cube. When this boils, add noodles and stir well, raking strands with a fork. Cook for 2 minutes and serve garnished with chopped spring onions. Typically, left-over chicken will be used.

Braised Rice Noodles
with Shrimps and Squid

Chinese noodles are made from wheat, rice or mung bean flour. Sold dry, or occasionally fresh in specialist stores, they need only be boiled or soaked till soft. Wheat noodles expand roughly to twice their bulk but rice and mung bean noodles do not.

8 oz/200 g rice noodles
1 clove garlic, crushed
2 tbsp vegetable oil
3 tbsp oyster sauce
10 fl oz/300 ml water
4 oz/100 g/½ cup beansprouts
3 oz/75 g raw shrimps
3 oz/75 g cleaned squid
½ tsp pepper
fresh coriander or spring onions, chopped

Cook noodles to packet Instructions adding 2 tbsp oil when boiling to prevent sticking. Drain. Clean and devein shrimps. Cut squid into ½ in/1 cm rings or 1 in/2½ cm square if large. Fry garlic in hot oil till light brown. Add oyster sauce and water and bring to the boil. Add shrimps and squid and cook for 1 minute. Add all other ingredients and stir well for about 2 minutes. Serve garnished with fresh coriander or chopped spring onions.

Yangzhou Jewel Rice

'Have you eaten rice?' is the traditional Chinese greeting, explaining its importance to the Chinese. Yangzhou (sometimes spelt Yang Chow) is the Eastern city in the Yang Tze region from which fried rice originated. It is a colourful mix of rice, ham, peas, carrots and egg, hence the jewel reference.

---

10 oz/250 g/1 cup long grain rice (enough water to cover 1 in/2½ cm above rice level)
4 tbsp oil
2 eggs, lightly beaten
6 oz/150 g cooked ham, cut into ¾ in/1 cm cubes
2 tbsp cooked green peas
2 carrots, cubed and blanched
1 vegetable stock cube, crumbled
spring onion stalks, chopped

Wash rice, add water and cook covered, over a medium heat for 10-12 minutes, until all water is absorbed. Switch off heat. Stir to loosen and allow to get completely cold. Heat oil and cook eggs until set. Add all other ingredients. Stir well to break up stock cube. Garnish with chopped spring onions.

Shrimp Dumpling Soup

From ancient times, Chinese people were fond of eating at tea houses. From these came a range of snacks now a permanent feature in most Chinese restaurants. A Dim Sum (literally 'to touch the heart') meal can be two or 200 dishes!

---

20 won ton pastry skins, each 2½ in/6 cms square
12 oz/300 g/minced pork
6 oz/150 g raw minced prawns
2 tsp cornflour
2 tbsp sesame oil
½ tbsp pepper
2 tbsp light soy sauce
2 oz/50 g translucent vermicelli, soaked till soft
30 fl oz/750 ml water
1 chicken stock cube
fresh coriander or spring onions, chopped

Mix pork, prawns, cornflour, sesame oil, pepper and soy sauce. Place 2 tsp on each won ton skin, gather up and twist to seal with a little water. Bring water and stock cube to boil. Drop in dumplings and vermicelli, cook for 3 minutes. Adjust seasoning. Garnish with fresh coriander or chopped spring onions.

Chicken Pancake Rolls

This is another Dim Sum item with more variations than leaves on a tree! Minced pork and cabbage is the classic filling but you can ring the changes with chicken and beansprouts or any shredded leafy vegetable.

---

6 spring roll skins 10 in/125 cms square
2 tbsp oil
2 cloves garlic, crushed
12 oz/300 g/¾ cup chicken breast, minced
12 oz/300 g/2 cups beansprouts
2 tbsp light soy sauce
1 tsp pepper
oil for deep-frying
3 tbsp sesame oil
cucumber, sliced

Heat oil and fry garlic until light brown. Add all other ingredients and stir-fry for 3 minutes until chicken is cooked. Allow to cool. If needed, defrost spring roll skins, keeping them covered with a damp tea towel to prevent cracking while working. Place 2 tbsp of mixture near the edge of skin. Roll over once, fold in sides and roll again to make a firm sausage. Seal edges with a little water and allow to sit for a few minutes. Add sesame oil to deep-fry oil for nutty fragrance. Deep-fry rolls until golden brown and serve with a chili sauce dip and sliced cucumbers.

Sesame Toast

Though a migrant snack in its use of bread, this is an hors d'oeuvre with lots of savoury crunch. Use a pastry cutter to make rounds of bread.

---

1 sandwich loaf with crust trimmed
12 oz/300 g/¾ cup minced pork
6 oz/150 g raw minced prawns
3 eggs, lightly beaten
2 tbsp light soy sauce
½ tsp pepper
8 oz/200 g/⅓ cup sesame seeds
oil for deep-frying

Mix pork, prawns and 2 tbsp of beaten egg with soy sauce and pepper. Cut bread into rounds about 1½ in/4 cm in diameter. With a pastry brush, lightly coat each round with egg and spread mixture about ¼ in/½ cm thick, patting down firmly. You should get between 20 and 24 pieces. Brush with more egg and coat with sesame seeds. Fry a few at a time until golden brown, turning once. Drain on absorbent paper.

Plum Sauce Chicken

Chinese chefs are master at making inexpensive ingredients look and taste wonderful. With a little work, humble chicken wings become imperial offerings. All it needs is patience, ingenuity and a sharp knife.

---

12 chicken wings, tips removed
2 eggs, lightly beaten
10 cream crackers, finely crushed
oil for deep frying
4 tbsp plum sauce
2 tbsp hoi sin sauce
cucumber rounds
pineapple rings

Cut away thin end of wing joint. Scrape down along the two bones until meat forms a thick ball at the other end. Shape firmly into little lollipops. Remove thin bone leaving thick one as a handle. Roll first in beaten egg and then in crushed crackers. Leave to settle for a few minutes before deep-frying until golden brown. Keep crisp in a warm oven. Serve on rounds of cucumber and pineapple rings with dips of plum and hoi sin sauce.

Pot Stickers

Legend has it that a forgetful chef burnt a batch of dumplings. His quick-witted son deflected the Emperor's wrath by saying his father had invented a special dish called 'pot stickers' with burnt bottoms. To further mask the fault, he served them with sharp vinegar and ginger sauce.

---

12 oz/350 g/3 cups plain flour, sifted
7 fl oz/250 ml/1 cup warm water
Filling
5 oz/100 g/1 cup shredded cabbage
10 oz/200 g/1 cup minced pork
1 oz/25 g/2 tbsp light soy sauce
½ tsp pepper
2 tbsp sesame oil
1 egg, lightly beaten
4 oz/100 g/5 tbsp oil for frying

Mix flour with the water and knead for 10 minutes until dough comes away from bowl. Rest dough. Blanch cabbage in boiling water for 2 minutes, drain and mix with other ingredients. Divide dough into 3 parts. Roll each into 10 in/25 cms length. Cut into 10 rings and roll each out into 3 in/7 cms round. Place 2 tsp of filling in each and shape into half moons, pinching each firmly to seal. Heat oil in a frying pan and lightly brown as many as you can at one time. Add 6 fl oz/180 ml/¾ cup water, cover and cook until the pan is dry and the bottom of each pot sticker is brown. To make the dip, mix 4 tbsp malt vinegar with 2 tbsp soy sauce and 2 tbsp finely shredded ginger.

Chinese Steamed Bun

This basic Chinese dough mix can also be wrapped around a multitude of fillings for delicious sweet or savoury dumplings. A north China staple (no rice is grown in this region) symbolising plenty, traditionally it is served steamed with savoury meat dishes.

1 lb/500 g/4 cups plain flour, sifted
1 oz/20 g/2 tbsp dried yeast
2 tsp sugar
3 tbsp lukewarm water
9 fl oz/300 ml/1 cup warm milk

Mix yeast, sugar and warm water. Leave in warm place till frothy. Pour this and warm milk into flour. Stir until firm dough is formed. Knead on a floured board for 15 minutes and leave in warm place until dough doubles. Knead for 5 minutes and roll into sausage shape about 1 in/2½ cms in diameter. Cut into 24 rounds and roll out each to 4 in/10 cms diameter. Fold over and lightly brush with oil. Rest for 20 minutes. Place on a wet cloth on a perforated steamer rack (bamboo is best) and steam for 20 minutes. Allow 1 in/2½ cm space between buns. Serve hot or cold.

Pork Dumplings

So revered is the dumpling in Chinese cuisine that there is a festival honouring it. They are given as offerings to Taoist deities and after prayers, villagers feast on them.

Dumpling dough (see page 20)
Filling
1 lb/500 g pork fillet
2 tbsp sugar
2 tbsp light soy sauce
3 tbsp honey
2 tbsp hoi sin sauce

Cut pork into strips about 1 in/2 cms thick. Steep in marinade ingredients for 30 minutes. Roast on a rack for 40 minutes in pre-heated oven at gas mark 6, 400°F 200°C. Cool and cut into ½ in/1 cm cubed dice. Knead proven dough for 5 minutes and roll into sausage shape about 1½ in/3½ cms diameter. Cut into 24 rounds. Flatten each till 4 in/10 cm diameter. Place 1 tbsp filling on each, draw up sides and twist at top to seal firmly. Steam as for plain dumplings for 20 minutes. Serve hot or cold. Vary the filling with chicken or beef.

Crab and Sweetcorn Soup

Chinese soups are generally served with a meal so diners may take sips to refresh the palate between mouthfuls. There are herbal soups like those with ginseng reputed to do the libido no end of good! This one is less exciting but very satisfying, especially on a cold winter's evening.

---

12 fl oz/370 g/1½ cups creamed sweetcorn
8 oz/250 g/½ cup crab meat
12 fl oz/375 ml water
3 tbsp sesame oil
2 tbsp light soy sauce
½ tsp pepper
2 eggs
fresh coriander, chopped
croutons

Beat eggs lightly and combine all ingredients in a soup pot. Bring to the boil and adjust seasoning to taste. Serve with croutons and chopped fresh coriander. To vary, use diced chicken or shrimps. More egg will give you a thicker, heartier soup.

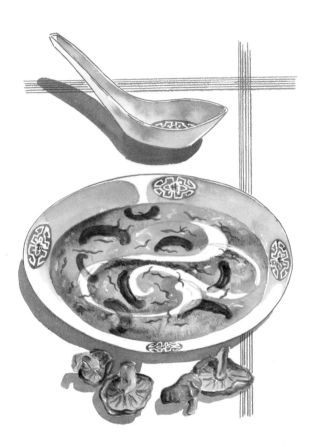

Egg Drop Mushroom Soup

Smoky-flavoured Chinese dried mushrooms are quite different from field mushrooms. They symbolise prosperity, especially those with fissures on the caps. These 'blossom' mushrooms can be expensive during festive seasons so use field mushrooms instead.

1½ pt/750 ml/3 cups water
1 vegetable stock cube
6 Chinese mushrooms, soaked in hot water till soft
1 tbsp shredded ginger
4 tbsp Chinese wine (Hsiao Hsing or Hwa Chiu)
3 tbsp seasme oil
2 eggs, lightly beaten
2 tbsp brandy

Bring stock cube and water to the boil. Snip off mushroom stalks and cut each top into strips. Add to stock together with ginger, wine and sesame oil. As the soup boils pour in beaten egg, gently swirling as you do. Just before serving add brandy.

Shrimp Fu Yong

To dine off Fu Yong is to augur a smooth path to prosperity, so say the Chinese. It is also good eating. The classic ingredients are egg and carrot with shrimps or crab.

---

5 eggs, lightly beaten
1 large carrot, grated
8 oz/250 g/½ cup raw shrimps or crab meat
3 tbsp oil
1 tbsp light soy sauce
2 stalks spring onions, chopped
1 tbsp sesame seeds
lettuce leaves

Clean and devein shrimps. Heat oil and fry carrot for 1 minute. Push aside and pour in beaten egg. Stir gently for 2 minutes as you would for scrambled eggs then add shrimps and soy sauce. Continue stirring until shrimps turn pink and Fu Yong is almost dry. Serve with chopped spring onions and sesame seeds sprinkled on top. The Chinese say that 'to eat sesame seeds is to have numerous progeny, a farmer's blessing of many hands to till the soil'. For an amusing starter, the Fu Yong can be wrapped in fresh lettuce leaves.

Spicy Sichuan Spare Ribs

There's nothing spare about Chinese ribs, if you can get your butcher to reserve some with plenty of meat on them. Get him to chop them up as you would need a heavy cleaver and some strength to hew through the bone. To make ribs succulent and tender, the trick is to parboil them in their marinade before deep frying.

---

2 lbs / 1 kg spare ribs, cut into 2 in/5 cms pieces
3 tbsp hoi sin sauce
2 tsp Sichuan peppercorns
4 tbsp sherry or Chinese wine
½ tsp five spice powder
1 pt/500 ml/2 cups water
oil for deep frying

Marinate ribs in all ingredients except water for 1 hour or overnight. Add water and bring to the boil. Cook for 20 minutes until liquid is reduced. Drain and cool. Heat oil until smoking and fry ribs for 2 minutes. Reduce marinade until thick and serve as a side dip. For less oily ribs you can also barbecue after boiling.

Drunken Chicken

This is believed to be a favourite of the Tang Dynasty Empress Yang Kwei Fei renowned for her beauty and her fondness for a tipple. Traditionally cooked in a clay pot, a Chinese chicken, served whole with its head, represents the Phoenix and rebirth. You wouldn't want to go to your other life headless!

---

1 chicken, about 3 lb/1.5 kg
6 tbsp oil
¼ pt/150 ml/⅓ cup Chinese wine or sherry
3 pt/1.7 ltr/7 cups water
4 tbsp light soy sauce
2 tbsp shredded ginger
4 tbsp sesame oil
2 cloves garlic, crushed

Mix 2 tbsp each of soy sauce and wine and rub over chicken. Turn chicken in heated oil until light brown. Transfer to a deep pot with all other ingredients and simmer for 1½ hours. Turn several times and add a little water or wine if necessary. Serve hot or cold with steamed buns. Most Chinese supermarkets sell clay pots. The clay imparts a smoky flavour to the dish and the pot, served straight from the stove, gives an authentic and rustic touch.

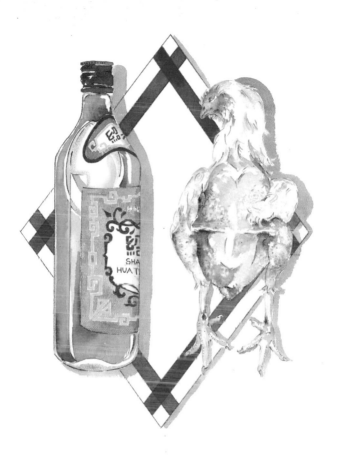

Soy Braised Chicken

You will see this Cantonese speciality hanging in most Chinese restaurants. Done well, it will have a mahogany sheen. Served with a sharp chili dip and plain rice it's positively ambrosial. It's practically a national lunch-time meal.

1 chicken, about 3 lb / 1.5 kg
4 tbsp oil
2 tbsp sugar
6 tbsp dark soy sauce
1 large knob ginger root, bruised
2 tsp salt
2 tbsp chopped onion

Heat oil and caramelise sugar until it is a dark brown but not burned. Add soy sauce and quickly turn chicken in it until well coated. Add water, ginger, salt and onion and simmer for 1 hour, turning several times. Cool and cut into pieces. Reduce sauce and serve with chicken. To make a quick chili dip, grind 4 fresh red chilies with 3 cloves of garlic and mix with 4 tbsp malt vinegar and 1 tsp salt.

Chicken and Cashew Nuts in Yellow Bean Sauce

The epitome of culinary balance in Chinese cuisine, this dish has a perfect blend of texture, shape, colour and flavour. It is easy to cook in either a wok or a frying pan.

---

3 tbsp oil
8 oz/250 g chicken breast, cubed
2 tbsp yellow bean sauce
1 red pepper, diced in ½ in/1 cm squares
1 stalk celery, diced as above
20 cashew nuts
1 tsp sugar
2 tbsp sesame oil
5 tbsp water

Heat oil and fry chicken for 1 minute till half cooked. Add yellow bean sauce and stir to blend. Add all other ingredients except water and stir-fry for 2 minutes. Add water, stir, and when mixture thickens remove from wok and serve hot.

Peking Duck

Aficionados wax lyrical about this splendid dish, even down to the merit of adding ducks' beaks! In Peking, some restaurants are devoted entirely to this dish and some books specify the type of oven and firewood to roast this princely dish. You will still dine with imperial grandeur, using a good Aylesbury duckling and store-bought Mandarin pancakes!

---

1 good sized duckling
2 tbsp honey diluted with a little water
Accompaniments
Mandarin pancakes (store-bought)
5 tbsp hoi sin sauce
4 stalks spring onions, cut into fine strips 2 in/5 cms long
1 cucumber, skinned, cored and cut into similar size

Hang duck overnight in a warm place, or on your clothesline in direct sunlight for 3-4 hours until skin is absolutely dry. The secret is to remove as much moisture as possible. A good blast all over with a hair-dryer does the job also. Pre-heat oven for 30 minutes at mark 6, 400°F, 200°C. Rub melted honey all over duck and roast on a rack for 40 minutes. Turn heat to medium and roast for a further 30 minutes. Remove duck, leave for 15 minutes. Allowing 4 or 5 pancakes for each person, steam a few at a time for 10 minutes and keep warm. Slice duck skin with a little meat into 2 in/5 cm squares. Paint each pancake with a little hoi sin sauce and place a few shreds of spring onions and cucumber in centre. Add a piece or two of duck skin and roll up. Most Chinese supermarkets sell pancakes, or tortillas will make a thicker substitute. Traditionally, the meat from the duck carcase will reappear as stir-fried duck with vegetables, and the bones will be boiled with another vegetable for soup.

Sweet and Sour Pork

'Fire and water, vinegar, pickle, salt and plums. Fire boils water and the cook orchestrates the harmony equalising flavours. Then the master eats and his mind is made equable', said a disciple of Confucius, circa 600 BC. It says everything about this famous Chinese export.

---

1 lb/500 g pork fillet in 1 in/2 cm cubes
2 eggs, lightly beaten
cornflour
oil for deep frying
½ onion, sliced
2 tomatoes, quartered
1 small can pineapple chunks, reserve juice
Sauce
3 tbsp plum sauce
3 tbsp tomato sauce
5 tbsp pineapple juice
1 tsp malt vinegar

Roll pork in egg, remove with a slotted spoon and coat with cornflour. Shake off excess and leave to settle. Deep fry till golden brown and set aside. Heat 3 tbsp oil and fry onions for 1 minute. Add sauce ingredients, pineapple and tomatoes and add pork when sizzling. Sauce should just coat pork. Add a little water for a thinner consistency. Serve with rice.

Braised Pork Belly

Any aversion to fat pork will change when you've tasted this sinfully rich dish. It's simply not the same made with lean pork. Plain steamed buns (see recipe on page 20) make a perfect foil for every juicy drop.

---

2 lb / 1 kg belly pork, cut into 3 or 4 pieces lengthwise
3 cloves garlic, crushed
4 tbsp dark soy sauce
1 tsp five-spice powder
5 tbsp Chinese wine
3 tbsp oil
1 tsp sugar
2 pt / 1 ltr water
fresh coriander

Marinate pork for an hour in garlic, soy sauce, five-spice powder and wine. Drain and seal well in hot oil. Add water and sugar and simmer for 1½ hours until pork is tender. Drain and slice. Reduce liquid and pour over sliced pork or serve in a gravy boat with steamed buns and fresh coriander.

Mongolian Lamb Stew

This is an ancient stew that was called Tung Po mutton by the 11th century Chinese Muslim poet, painter and epicure of the same name. Sometimes goat meat is used, but lamb will do just as well.

---

1 lb/500 g stewing lamb, trimmed of fat
6 oz/150 g potatoes, each cut in four
4 oz/100 g carrot, cut into ½ in/1 cm chunks
2 tbsp/30 ml soy sauce
1 tsp/20 g ground ginger
1 tsp/15 g five-spice powder
½ tsp black pepper
6 tbsp/100 ml oil
5 tbsp rice wine

Cut lamb into 1 in/2½ cm pieces. Pat dry and seal well in hot oil. Remove lamb from pan, and fry potatoes and carrots for 5 minutes. Remove and set aside. Put lamb and seasoning ingredients in a deep pot and add water to 1 in/2½ cm above ingredients. Bring to the boil and simmer for 2 hours. Add potatoes, carrots, and rice wine 5 minutes before end of cooking time.

Steamed Sea Bass

This is possibly the most magnificent and easily prepared fish dish.
If you cannot get sea bass, use fresh snapper, grouper or halibut.

2 lb/1 kg sea bass, cleaned and gutted but with head left on
2 tbsp shredded ginger
3 Chinese mushrooms, soaked and cut into strips
2 tbsp light soy sauce
1/2 tsp black pepper
4 tbsp/50 ml sherry
2 tbsp oil
spring onions, chopped

Score fish diagonally several times almost to the bone. Place on a
plate deep enough to contain steamed juices. Press ginger and
mushroom strips into crevices. Dribble over soy sauce, oil, pepper
and sherry. Cook for 10 minutes in a steamer with a porous lid
(bamboo or perforated metal). Sprinkle with chopped spring
onions. Any left-over liquid makes a lovely stock base.

Stir~Fried Prawns and Mange Tout

The southern Chinese say that 'to eat prawns is to augur well for a happy life'. The word for prawns in the Cantonese dialect is 'ha' as in laughter. Since other Chinese words for prawns do not translate similarly, the belief doesn't apply outside this province.

---

4 tbsp oil
12 large fresh prawns, peeled
1 tsp sugar
4 oz/125 g mange tout, topped and tailed
1 clove garlic, crushed
1 tbsp light soy sauce
2 tbsp sesame oil
fresh coriander

Marinate prawns in sugar for an hour. Heat oil and fry crushed garlic till light brown. Add prawns and mange tout and fry rapidly over high heat for 1 minute. Add seasoning and stir for another minute. Serve immediately, garnished with sprigs of fresh coriander.

Steamed Cabbage Rolls

When cabbage is mentioned in Chinese cooking it can mean the Savoy type or the Winter variety, known in this country as Chinese leaf. This recipe refers to the latter, now widely available and with a sweeter taste.

---

8 cabbage leaves
8 oz/250 g minced pork
6 oz/150 g minced raw prawns
1 tsp salt
1 tsp cornflour
½ tsp pepper
1 egg, lightly beaten
shallots or garlic, fried

Boil a pot of water and blanch leaves of equal size until soft but not mushy. Drain and set aside. Mix pork, prawns and seasoning with egg. Taste for seasoning. Place 2 tbsp of mixture on each leaf and roll up firmly. Steam rolls on a plate for 10 minutes. Serve hot with their own juices garnished with fried shallots or garlic.

The 18 Lohan

The name of this dish, revered by Buddist vegetarians, refers to the 18 disciples of the Lord Buddha whose Sanskrit name is Lohan. Here are the original 18 ingredients but anything up to six gives a satisfying result unless you're a purist: Chinese leaf, dry mushrooms, straw mushrooms, hairy mushrooms, cloud ears, white fungus, mange tout, sweet tofu wafers, brown tofu, red dates, gingko nuts, lotus seeds, translucent vermicelli, hair vegetable, lily buds, preserved bean cured, hoi sin sauce, garlic.

---

6 mange tout, topped and tailed
2 Chinese cabbage leave, slice into 1 in/2 cms pieces
6 French beans, topped and tailed
6 Chinese mushrooms, soaked till soft and stalks cut off
12 button mushrooms
20 lily buds (golden needles), soaked till soft and hard tips cut off. Tie each into a knot
1 cube preserved red bean curd, mashed
2 tbsp hoi sin sauce
2 tbsp soy sauce
1 tsp pepper
4 tbsp oil
½ pt/250 ml cup water

Heat oil and blend with preserved bean curd. Add hoisin sauce and stir for 1 minute. Drain and dry vegetables and add to all other ingredients except water and stir. Add water and cook over high heat, stirring constantly until thick. This dish tastes even better the next day.

Almond Lychee Surprise

It's a fallacy to think Chinese do not have a sweet tooth, though desserts are not usually served after a meal rather as in-between snacks. In fact, sugar is revered and the icon of the kitchen diety is always smeared with sugar water so that he will give good reports in Heaven about the household!

---

2 sachets unflavoured gelatin (2 tbsp each)
1 pt/500 ml/2 cups water
5 tbsp sugar
8 fl oz/250 ml/1 cup milk
1 tbsp almond essence
1 large can lychees

Stir gelatine in half the water and sugar until dissolved. Boil the remaining water and pour into gelatin mixture. Stir until mixture is clear. Blend milk with almond essence and add to mixture. Pour into jelly mould and refrigerate when cool. To serve, either arrange lychees around whole jelly or cut up and serve in individual dishes. Any tinned fruit can be used.

Golden Bites

Butter is rarely, if ever, used in Chinese desserts and I suspect this pudding came to China by way of Far East migrants who enjoyed imported New Zealand butter.

Pastry
2 oz/50 g/¼ cup butter
2 oz/50 g/¼ cup lard
I egg
6 tbsp sugar
8 oz/250 g/2 cups sifted flour
Filling
4 large eggs, half the white discarded
¾ pt/400 ml/1½ cups milk
10 oz/300 g/1 cup sugar

Cream butter with lard and add egg and sugar. Beat well and add flour. Stir till dough is firm. Knead for 10 minutes and set aside. Beat eggs until blended but not frothy. Add sugar and milk and stir over a bowl of warm water. Leave for 15 minutes. Separate dough into 20 balls and press each into a shallow ramekin to form a tart shell making sure thickness is even. Fill each with egg mixture and bake in pre-heated oven at gas mark 4, 300°F, 150°C for 40 minutes. Cool and unmould.

Goreng Pisang

This is an exotic way to treat bananas and it's practically a national snack among migrant populations in Southeast Asia who serve it with scoops of coconut or mango ice cream.

---

8 bananas, peeled
3 oz/70 g/½ cup self-raising flour
3 oz/70 g/½ cup rice flour
1 tbsp cornflour
½ pt/250 ml/1 cup water
½ tsp salt
4 tbsp fine brown sugar
oil for deep frying

Slice each banana lengthways into two. Sift flours and add to water. Stir until consistency of cream. Add salt. Heat oil and when smoking, dip each piece of banana in batter, shake off excess and lower into hot oil. Fry until golden brown and roll in brown sugar. Serve with ice cream.

Index